ALONG THE WOOD

Mary Rose Hayfield's Country Poetry

For Harry with Love

Mary Rose Hayfield

CONTENTS

	Page
Title Page	1
Contents Page	2
In April in the Lane	3
Retirement	4 and 5
Ettington W.I.	6 and 7
Snowdrops	8
Lily Dale	9
Gelli Farm	10 and 11
A Lawn Newmown	12
Corley	13
The Nestbox	14
Radway, under Edge Hill	15
Silver Wedding	16 and 17
Aston Cantlow	18
A Loved One Lost	19
Ilmington	20
Forgiveness	21
Golden Gift for a Child	22 and 23
Love	24
Chipping Campden Church	25
Forever Young	26
For a Daughter	27
Aberaeron	28 and 29
Litter	30
Village Schools	31
My Sister and I	32 and 33
Rowan Hayfield	34
Little Shrewley	35
Appleby Magna and Appleby Parva	36
Fairies	37
Spring Comes Late to the Mountains	38
Country Childhood	39
Little Things	40 and 41
Who Cares?	42
Daffodils Blowing	43
Baddesley Clinton	44 and 45
Exhall in may	46
Open your Eyes	47
My Garden	48

IN APRIL IN THE LANE

In April in the cottage lane
The catkins dance and dance again,
Above the tiny winding stream
Remembered in a Winter's dream.

The oak trees all along the meadow
Cast then a little leafy shadow,
Where primrose bud and dainty flower
Enchant again the witching hour.

The robin and the tiny wren
Begin to sing sweet songs again,
The woodland floor is brown and bare
But bluebell spears are greening there.

The April showers pass quickly by
And rainbows spill across the sky,
And there beneath my wandering feet
White violets scented, pale and sweet.

And in the hazel catkin bush
There sings the speckled missel thrush,
Who soon will build her twiggy nest
Deep in the old oak's ivied breast.

Beyond my little garden hedge
The lane, the field, the stream, the sedge,
Are dressing up in softest green
As Spring transforms dark Winter's scene.

Of all the joys each year can bring
Surely the greatest must be . . . Spring

RETIREMENT

"Time to smell the roses."

So many memories
Years passing by,
Look over your shoulder
How time can fly.

Working life gathered
Days into years,
Meetings and partings
The joys and the tears.

Experience and pleasure
Cast the net wide,
Working life ended
Lay it aside.

Hard to relinquish
Closing the book,
Farewell to old friendships
Take a last look.

Hours to be peaceful
And gather life's posies,
Time now for resting
And smelling the roses.

May your future be happy
Whatever you do,
Your friends and old comrades
Raise glasses to you.

But when a door closes
Another is wide,
And you will go bravely
To see what's inside.

Let the world see you smiling
Dont envy the young,
In armchairs by the fireside
Dear memories grow strong.

A new life beginning
Each dawn a new day,
Retirements the pathway
Paving your way.

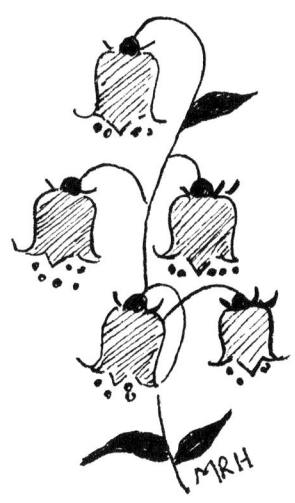

ETTINGTON W.I.

When we moved in at Ettington
The Monday, it was fine,
And I was in the garden
Pegging on the line.

Neighbour, just over the fence
Was sprinkling watering can,
And that I have to tell you
Was how it all began.

"Lovely day," says she to me
Before I can reply
She's THERE, up close beside me
"YOU MUST JOIN THE W.I.

"It's no use moping here you know
And getting in a rut,
The first Monday in every month
We meet down at the hut."

The first few months were Jolly D
Because I was so new,
I made some lovely friends you know
And won the raffle too.

Then all of a sudden
Don't know how it came to be,
But I was in the Drama Group
And helping make the tea.

"You needn't do the Can Can
In frilly pants and pearls,
Just wear these old red bloomers
And make eyes at the girls".

It all went right upon the night
And on the up and upper,
Till Madam Drama said to me
"Encore for Harvest Supper".

My knees then turned to water
My pulse began to flicker,
How could I wear red bloomers
In front of our dear Vicar?

But very shortly after that
I went on the Committee,
Coffee mornings, Jumble Sales
And all that nitty gritty.

"If you could take the minutes,
Miss Jones, she is not able,
And how about a posy
For Madam President's table?

One year I planned the Programme
I didn't get it right,
I booked some lovely speakers
But all on the wrong night.

I also ran the Outings
And correctly booked the dates
But we set off with twenty-six
And came back with twenty-eight.

This year I've been the President
And now I must confess,
I'm having such a georgeous year
It has to be success.

SNOWDROPS

In Wales long ago

When the River Aeron's frozen
Banks encrusted, scrolls of snow,
All the streambed rocks are icebound
East wind through the woodland blow.

Old woodland overhangs the steam bank
Icicles hang every bough,
Bracken floor of woodland frozen
Squirrels sleeping, blood runs slow.

Woodland birds strive for a living
Old buzzard gloomy, swoops down low,
Yet beneath the dead leaves lying
A million bulbs beneath the snow.

And when days begin to lengthen
Snow and ice to melt away,
A million bulbs begin their striving
Push towards the light of day.

Snow has gone and green the meadow
Old Aeron free, flows on his way,
Beneath the trees, a thousand, thousand,
Dainty snowdrops nod and sway.

Oh the magic of that woodland,
Before old Aeron meets the sea,
There's never been so loved a Springtime
As those dear snowdrops gave to me.

LILY DALE

Of Cosyl Cottage, Coleshill

The Tailor Bird
1930 – 1950

Oh Lily Dale was more to me
Than others I have known,
She showed me all the country ways
When I was scaresely grown.

She showed me where the primrose grew
Beneath the hazel bough
And violets by the mossy path
No cottage stands there now.

And on the bank beside the stream
She lifted me to see
The mallard's nest all lined with down
Within the hollow tree.

She showed me how to sew fine seams
Embroider tiny flowers
Across Dole meadows cowslip path
We spent such happy hours.

Though Lily Dales forgotten
And sixty years flown free,
Dear grey haired maiden lady
Yet still she walks with me.

Along the lanes of Maxstoke
And footpaths in the meadows,
I walk with memories hand in hand
With Lily Dale's dear shadow.

GELLI FARM

Talsarn, near Lampeter in Ceredigion.

And still across the marsh to me
Comes sad and lonely curlew call,
Beyond the cowshed in the tree
The wood-owl watches darkness fall.

And though I am so far away
I know the larks are rising still,
Above where meadow grasses sway
Above the hayfield on the hill.

And in the garden near the stream
The warbler nests in hidden hole,
I close my eyes and I can dream
Of Patsy donkey's new born foal.

And there the ponies by the gate
With velvet noses wait for me,
They're looking for a bowl of cake
And telling me it's time for tea.

I wonder do the red kite rare
Still fly above the Aeron Vale?
We only ever saw one pair
Red of wing and forked of tail.

Beneath the beech do squirrels still
Hurl empty beech masts to the ground?
Wild daffodils with yellow frill
Still carpet woodland all around.

In Spring do young lambs frisk around
About the mossy fallen tree?
The burbling stream a lovely sound
With gurgling song for you and me.

Oh how I long to go again
Along the grassy, mossy track,
To laugh beneath soft falling rain
And hear wood-peckers laughing back.

To be among the wildest ways
Where polecat walk beneath the moon,
Where fox and badger live their days
And morning never comes too soon.

To see each day the sun rise high
And know I am once more at home,
To hear again sad curlew's cry
And know my heart to rest has come.

A LAWN NEWMOWN

I saw the marks where you had mown
The lawn, but yet a week ago,
Long covered now by rain and snow,
And frosty rime of Winter days.
And yet to me the sadness still,
Is lingering on of that sad day;
When death with such a gentle hand,
Came soft, and carried you away.
Away without a last goodbye,
Beyond the farthest far beyond.
And now the grass so recent mown,
Brings back your memory deep and strong.

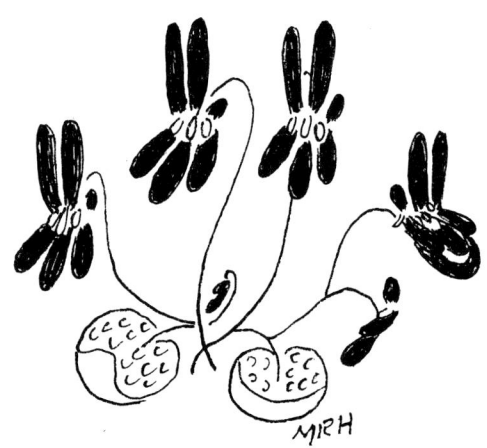

CORLEY

Corley stands upon a hill
Where Warwickshire is lovely still,
Her Church which Normans helped to build
Her trees, low branches overspilled.

Though Coventry is near at hand
Yet Corley still is "Country Land",
Where field and cottage garden hide
Beloved by owners, held with pride.

No motorway nor modern stress
Can touch or hurt the trees that bless,
The Churchyard in this country place
Where life moves gentle . . . slower pace.

And down the hill stand Corley Rocks
Where ancient Britains lived and rocked,
Rough hewn out cradles long ago
Ancestors we can never know.

All round the village, farm and field
For centuries give up their yield,
Of wheat, potatoes, oats and corn
Passed on to farmer's sons unborn.

May all the Corley village folk
For peaceful village life style work,
May God hold in his gentle hand
Your farms, your Church, this precious land.

THE NESTBOX

Bluetits in the nest box
Beyond the window still,
Like little acrobats they're building
Moss, and twigs and feathers fill.

Honeysuckle firmly twining
All around the next box hide,
Cosy little family dwelling
Moss lined nest is safe inside.

The little birds are flying freely
Dawn till dusk the live long day,
Twigs and moss and leaves and feathers
All they neatly weave away.

Soon the hen-bird will be sitting,
Lays a clutch of tiny eggs,
Patient waiting for their hatching
Ugly babies! Heads and legs!

Busy are the days that follow
Parent birds work all day long,
To and fro to feed their babies
Helping them grow big and strong.

Watching from within the window
Oh the joy! To see them fly,
Through the hazels and the birches,
Blue wings flutter . . . then Goodbye!

RADWAY

Under Edge Hill

April is the month for showers
Cottage gardens full of flowers,
Watched over by the Old Round Tower
    That stands on old Edge Hill.

Little narrow village lane
Daffodils blooming after rain,
Spring comes to Radway once again
    Under Old Edge Hill.

St Peters Church bells ringing
All the birds are singing,
Sun and showers are bringing
    Spring to Old Edge Hill.

Hillside slopes are clothed with trees
And village folk watch, as the leaves,
Unfurl and open in the breeze
    That blows on Old Edge Hill.

And in the village, hearts are lifting
Watching nature gently shifting,
The dark of Winter now is drifting
    Away from Old Edge Hill.

The Radway folk in village meeting
Each to each a friendly greeting,
And in the meadow, lambs are bleeting
    Spring for Old Edge Hill.

So lovely in the month of May
This village that is hid away,
Let quiet and peace forever stay
    Under Old Edge Hill.

SILVER WEDDING

Memories of your precious wedding day
When first you started out along your way,
The silver moonlight of your first romance
Soft welded now to move in slower dance.

Memories looking back across the years
Memories shared of joy, and love, and tears.
Memories woven rope of silver strand
Gathered close since first you took her hand.

Memories spanning twenty-five long years
Memories holding all your hopes and fears,
Memories threading silver in your hair
Your lives together only two could share.

Memories glowing pictures in your hearts
To share and keep whenever you're apart,
The silvered joy of every man and wife
"Forget-me-nots" of every happy life.

Memories of holidays and home
Memories of those dear years now gone,
The silver petalled roses of your dreams
That float upon the trauma of life's stream.

How fast the time of memory slips away
Bourne on the wings of every passing day,
The jewels of life set in a silver band
Twenty-five dear years in silver strand.

A silver milestone of the years before
The mirrored hope of golden years in store,
The rose flowers and the fruits of life's sweet wine
From silver threads, thick rope of silver twine.

Our silver wedding, this our happy days,
What we hold safe . . . no one can take away.

ASTON CANTLOW

Aston Cantlow willows weeping
Squirrels in their tree-holes sleeping,
Snow and ice on ponds are keeping
Cantlow's bitter Winter cold.

Aston Cantlow's gardens growing
Daffodil's golden petals blowing,
Farmers in the fields are sowing
And Aston Cantlow's Spring is here.

Aston Cantlow's Summer meadows
Churchyard trees cast gentle shadows,
Hamlet neighbours, Alne and Pathlow
Bask in Summers noonday sun.

Old house and cottage, nothing grand
St Johns Church here in beauty stand,
Where Shakespeare's parents hand in hand
Were married long ago.

In Autumn fields of harvest gold
And hedgerows, scarlet berried, bold,
Then Aston Cantlow folk behold
That glorious Autumns here.

Though village school is closed and gone
This lovely village still lives on,
Long may the sun still shine upon
The folk of Aston Cantlow now.

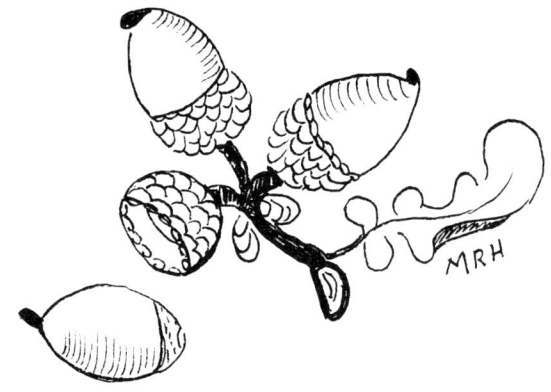

A LOVED ONE LOST

Gone from me from here to nowhere
Vanished like a puff of wind,
Lost forever from my seeing
Light as thistledown dear friend.

Loved one vanished, slipped from vision
Out of sight beyond the hill,
In my heart forever with me
Dear hand on my shoulder still.

Paths we trod, grass-grown forgotten
Words we said grow pale and fade,
And yet I know that you are waiting
Along the laneside in the shade.

Time itself is but a moment
Sunlit shadows on the road,
Wide your arms for me are waiting
Shed the burden of life's load.

ILMINGTON

A lovely village, open space
And life lived at a gentler pace,
Stone cottages and houses here
With grassy banks and spaces clear.

Old gardens here, with old stone walls
And manor house with chimneys tall,
The gardens full of cottage flowers
Where country folk pass happy hours.

Church and Church-yard, ancient trees
Old lavender and bumble bees,
Remembered now this lovely scene
And tea parties with Mrs Green.

The scent of blossom on the May
In Summer, fields of new mown hay,
The Ilmington that I remember
And apples ripening in September.

The Catholic Church, a wedding day
Sweet garden flowers, the bride's bouquet,
The tiny Church with love was filled
The family's happiness over-spilled . . .

Into Ilmington's village lane
And now when I go back again,
The sun and showers of memory carried
That precious day . . . when Pam was married.

FORGIVENESS

Hold hands within the family
Let not your anger grow,
For all disputes are trivial
And only love should flow.

No matter that we quarrel
Let's lay it all aside,
Lay hurt and grief away now
Forgiveness be the bride.

Let old wrongs be forgotten
Drive bitterness from your heart,
Don't let old words of anger
Tear families apart.

Hold fast the strands of family
That parents now long gone,
May know in their quiet Heaven
The family still lives on.

Mothers, sisters, children, babes
Hold hands with one another,
For all of us have heavy loads
So share it with your brother.

Let the baby born to Mary
In the manger long ago,
With smiles and friendship see his children's
Love within the family grow.

GOLDEN GIFT FOR A CHILD

Keep for the children
The memories we hold,
Cloud trails of glory
Dreams made of gold.

Keep space for the cowslip
To seed on the bank,
Old ponds of our childhood
Where wild creatures drank.

Don't gather the orchid
Grows shy in the lane,
The flowers carry seed-heads
They wont come again.

Blown thistles are seeding
The goldfinch grows rare,
And high on the mountain
The red-kite his share.

Drive safe for the badger
The polecat, the deer,
Bright lights in the darkness
Can fill them with fear.

A garden of buddleia
Scented and free,
Food for the butterfly
Wine for the bee.

Cow parsley and foxglove,
The gorse and the ling,
Give home to the skylark
And partridge in Spring.

Dig gentle your garden
Leave space that grows wild
For coltsfoot and cowslip
Are gifts for a child.

First glimpse of the rainbow
Child's magic delight,
Full moon hanging golden
On the wings of the night.

For we are the guardians
And in our hands hold,
This gift for our children
This treasure of gold.

LOVE

A love of passion
Passes swift away,
Fading, as starlight fades
At dawn of day;
But when real love is seen,
It's golden gleams,
Fill all the heart and mind
With peaceful dreams.
The kind of love that when all passion's spent
And daily work's a trial,
Extends fond arms and tender words to you,
That you may rest awhile.
A love that finds no sacrifice too great,
No time can alter,
The love that faces parting, pain and sorrow,
And does no falter.
This then is love beyond all rough-shod passion,
Enduring for ever.
A warm dear thing, so richly to be prized,
That fadeth never.

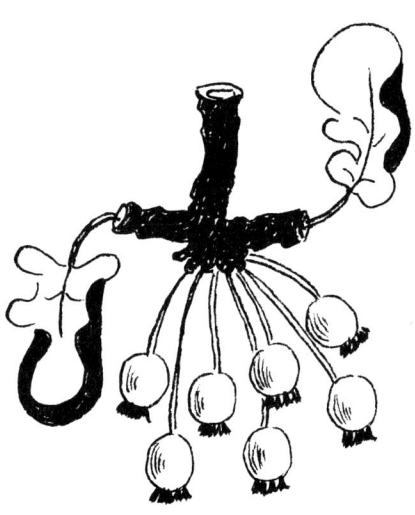

CHIPPING CAMPDEN CHURCH

Beloved Church whose golden stone
Glows warmly in the sun,
With a little path to a little door
Where the little choir-boys run.

Your tower serene, square to the wind
Stands there among the trees,
Worn flight of steps to wrought iron gates
With lawns about to please.

In early morn when near at hand
Some darkness till remains,
The pink-tipped fingers of the dawn
Gild soft your weather vane.

Your yew-lined walk inviting leads
To wide green fields below,
In Summer-time with daisies decked
In Winter, white with snow.

Your stout stone walls stand firm on guard
Above the green turf where loved ones rest,
And Spring-time comes and every year
With daffodils your graves are dressed.

The babies come at christening time
And bridces in white array,
The faithful follow, week by week
And visitors come day by day.

But you at peace eternal stand
By all the Campden folk adored,
Safe keep them each, and every heart,
Peace, faith and hope and love restored.

FOREVER YOUNG

Live always young!
And for the new, new day,
Dont count the years
Just let them slip away.

Dont give in to birthdays
The aches and pains of age,
Look for all the sunshine
And the flowers on life's sweet stage.

Give love and joy
To those you love the best,
And friendship and a smile
To all the rest.

For in their joy
You'll surely find your own,
In their young eyes
New happiness will come.

Show to the little ones
Life's lovely strings of pearls,
Give time and care to,
Little boys and girls.

Hedgehogs in the garden
Tadpoles in the pond,
Daddy-long-legs on the window
Bluebells in the wood beyond.

These the miracles of childhood
The primrose and the bumble-bee,
All these little country pleasures
You can give the children free.

The daisy and the robin's nest
Seen through the children's eyes,
All your years will slip away
Under their clear blue skies.

FOR A DAUGHTER

Remembered dearest baby long ago
A gift to make our marriage live and glow,
Remembered little girl in dainty dress
A toddler growing up our lives to bless.

Remembered as a child, first days in school
You grew so fast, away from our home rule,
Remembered as a teenager gone mad,
A few grey hairs for your old Mum and Dad.

Remembered first day that you forsook our home
Wild oats to sow and all the world to roam,
Remembered when you came back to our hearts
Our lovely daughter, never more to part.

Remembered on your happy wedding day,
Your Dad so proud in giving you away,
Remembered now with babies of your own,
Full circle has our dearest daughter come.

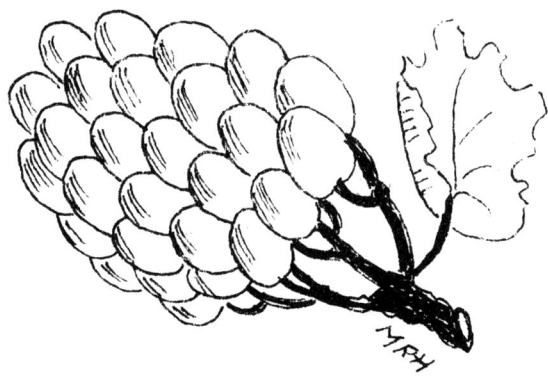

ABERAERON

Soft green fields slope gently down
To Aberaeron, dear old town,
Red and blue, and pink and green
The house fronts watch the harbour scene.

So quiet now and pace quite slow
When Summer visitors come and go,
First came the harbour years ago
Where ships to trade passed to and fro.

In history now when town began
And Alban Gwynne brought forth his plan,
Harbour, quaysides, piers of stone
A master plan, one man's alone.

Wide streets of Georgian houses here
Round grassy square, that's still kept clear,
Lovely houses, built to last
Each one a gem from time gone past.

There Beryl House and Aeron Queen
Lovely house names, fit the scene,
And Quay Parade leads to the sea,
Where Teashop serves a good cream tea.

Here green fields gentle cloak the town
And footpath follows Aeron down,
And lovers walk the river path
And roads leads on to Aberarth.

And Aberystwyth in the north
But such is Aberaeron's worth,
Where all the buildings blend so well
Church and Chapel, School on hill.

Old Aberaeron, dear to me
A Welsh gemstone, beside the sea,
Never forget old Alb an Square
The heart of Wales is beating there.

LITTER

Litter lying on the verges
Keeps no faith with England's pride,
Mr Everyman who throws it
Does not love his country-side.

Nature showers on us her promise
Flowers and buds beside the stile,
Let not litter so dispoil her
Do not your countryside defile.

Nature's tears wash down the hedgerows
Wild rose and honeysuckle bloom,
Nature sweeps away man's damage
With patient never ending broom.

VILLAGE SCHOOLS

Smooth worn stone steps,
A thousand feet,
Across the generations meet.
Where children passing
To and fro,
Have grown to women long ago.
Where little boys
Now grown to men,
Struggled with sums
And letters then;
And learned to spell
And laughed together,
And kicked a ball
In sunlit weather.
Their echoed voices
Still recall
Their childhood dreams
At village schools.
The trees, the Church,
The sun and shade,
The garden that
The children made.
Scattered perhaps
Across the world,
Bright young faces,
Lives unfurled.
But memory fades
The years away,
And village school
Seems yesterday.
Those village children
Far and near,
Still hold
Their village school most dear.

MY SISTER AND I

For Heather

The garden was our oyster
And Granny's flowers our pearls,
Within her cottage garden
When we were two little girls.

The little mossy stairway
Old oak with branches spread,
Our playhouse in the hollow tree
With dried leaves for a bed.

The orchard by the meadow
Where overhangs the stream,
An old red Worcester Apple
Low branch to sit and dream.

The oak tree was our kingdom
Oak-apples picked in Spring,
And acorns in their thousands
Our Autumn joy would bring.

Acorns, nuts and berries
We gathered for our house,
And no doubt in the Winter
Made food for sleepy mouse.

We picked the sprigs of lavender
And mixed them in our bed
Ate handfuls of wild raspberries
That grew behind the shed.

In Winter we made snowmen
Stream pebbles for their eyes,
Old hat and pipe from Grandad
Completed their disguise.

The stream was full of water-cress
Fresh-picked to eat for tea,
And Granny brought a rug for us
To picnic neath the tree.

Within that cottage garden
Two children's lives unfurled,
Such happiness remembered
When we were little girls.

ROWAN HAYFIELD

Lively wriggling little boy
Sent to be Grandmother's joy,
Never still from morn till night
Always giving us a fright.

Climbs on this and pushes that
Shrieks of joy and chase that cat,
Toys all thrown out through the door
Cupboard contents on the floor.

Build his bricks into a tower
All knocked down in noisy shower,
His dinner plate comes hurling after
Can children really burst with laughter?

Cheeky face with two bright eyes
Good as gold . . . no it's disguise,
Angelic saucy little smile
The birds from out the trees beguile.

Up the stairs on hands and knees
Like a monkey in the trees,
Come carefully down the stairs,
Do mind,
Bumps down each step on round behind.

Then quiet at night, small sleepy head,
In dreamless sleep curled up in bed,
Oh never failing source of joy
Most special, dearest little boy.

LITTLE SHREWLEY

A Warwickshire Gem

Little Shrewley, oh so dear
Green leafy Warwickshire is here,
Field and woodland, old oak tree
Unspoiled by time, so dear to me.

Pin Factory and Grinding Mill long gone
But now again the mill lives on,
Pine furniture and books rebound
In Shrewley's Craft Centre are found.

Along the lane under the tree
The foxgloves hang with bumble-bee,
And through the cottage garden gate
The scent of lavender, flowering late.

But village life here gently hums
And every Spring the Cuckoo comes,
And daffodils bloom at cottage door
And squirrels dance the woodland floor.

This village quiet and peaceful stand
All England's joy is here at hand,
A winding lane, house old, house new
Each with it's oak-leaved country view.

And though some folk have moved from town
And village life turned upside down,
Yet Shrewley still is country born
And birdsong fills her every dawn.

As long as Shrewleys life can be
So dear to such as you and me,
On tree and lane the sun will shine
And England still is yours and mine.

APPLEBY MAGNA AND APPLEBY PARVA

Gentle villages, modest, shy
Bustling busy world pass by,
In Spring your orchards blossom fill
And cottage garden daffodils.

In Summer fields on every side
Golden acres far and wide,
The farms of Leicestershire are here
Big fields of wheat and oats draw near.

Within the village Moat House stands
Well tended by most loving hands,
Sir Thomas More built this dear old
  school
His statue there recalls his rule.

And here the alms-houses still stand
A lovely place to live . . . not grand,
Timeless old buildings take their ease
The Old Black Horse is one of these.

And as I move along the street,
The Maypole Dancers tapping feet,
Are there, as though a long lost dream
Has lingered into modern scene.

Two magic villages are these
With gentle music on the breeze,
I stand and gaze, and drink my fill,
Unspoiled by time this village still.

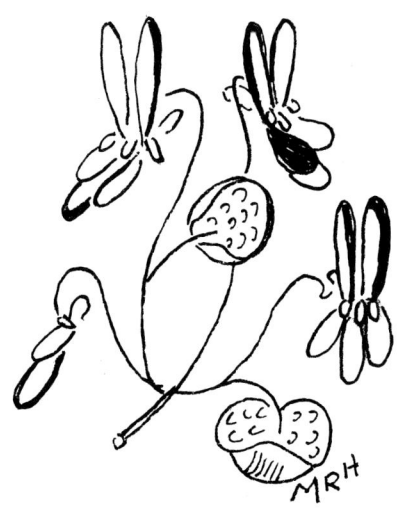

FAIRIES

Fairies fill our hearts with joy
Elves for every girl and boy,
Fairies leave the bathroom tidy
After children's baths on Friday.

Fairies and the little elf
Put books back neatly on the shelf,
Fairies, after making sweets
Leave Mummy's kitchen clean and neat.

Fairies put the toys away
After playing all long day,
Fairies down the garden play
But put the balls and bat away.

Fairies brush their pearly teeth
Never cause their Mother grief,
Fold their wings and tuck their heads
Into their downy thistle beds.

Fairies dancing on the lawn
Old as time and yet newborn,
Picking daisies in the rain
Before the lawn is mown again.

Fairies at the rainbow's end
Blown kisses to the children send,
And do our children fairies see?
Invisible to you and me.

How very lovely it would be
If children just like them could be,
And follow all the fairy ways
As good as gold through childhood days.

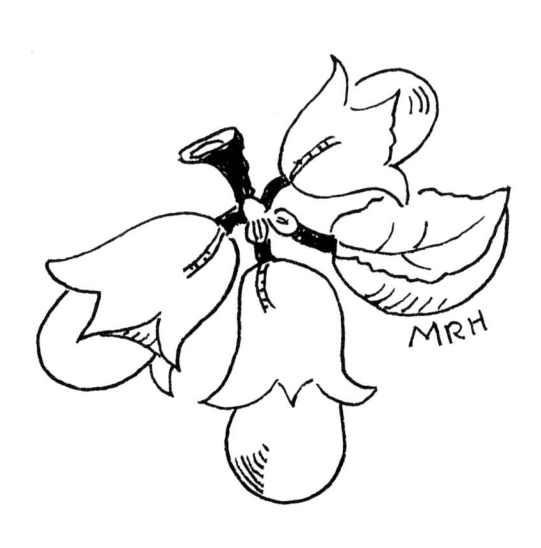

SPRING COMES LATE TO THE MOUNTAINS

I saw the shepherd yesterday
Upon the hill, three fields away,
He climbed the hill with easy stride
Towards the open mountain side.
The golden gorse hugs close the hill
But Springtime's frost is whitening still,
Where ancient sheep track winds away
Up there the lonely buzzards cry.
There's bitter cold, and lambs may die,
Save for the shepherd's watchful eye,
He'll bring them safely home.
A young lamb folded in his arm
The old ewe follows . . . no, alarm,
Into the barn and hay filled manger
Safe there until the lambs grows stronger.
Only the lonely shepherd sees
The leaf-buds on the rowan trees,
And knows that Spring is on his way
And sun grows stronger every day.
In his minds eye, the shepherd sees
Two hundred lambs beneath the trees,
Frolicing, playing round the fold
Brought safely through last Winter's cold.

COUNTRY CHILDHOOD

Born in the country
Down grassy lane,
Ancient thatched cottage
One tap, and no drain.

Low darkened doorway
Red tiled old floor
Red curtained small windows
Paint peeled old door.

Black leaded old range there
With mantle above,
Glowing coals in the hearth-place
Remembered with love.

Low beam in the bedroom
Old shabby armchair,
Soft feather bed cosy
Two sisters to share.

Wake early each morning
Run down twisting stair,
Boiled eggs in the kitchen
And Mother was there.

Games in the garden
Old bent apple trees,
Wrens nest in the ivy
Old hive full of bees.

Crusty bread with warm honey
Dear memories like pearls,
Tea times in the cottage
When we were small girls.

HRH

LITTLE THINGS

The little things
That when we roam,
The little things
That draw us home.

The little oak door
In the pantry wall,
That leads back in
The low beamed hall.

The little window
On the stairs,
The wooded hill
Is seen from there.

Fat acorns spread
The woodland floor,
The children gathered
Long before.

Old stream where
Water-cress grows thick,
That Grandad reached for
With his stick.

The clump of snowdrops
Every Spring,
Beside the gate
That's tied with string.

Leads to the meadow
Through the hedge,
Where west winds blow
The browning sedge

Bright golden kingcups
Flower in March,
That hug the stream
By bridge's arch.

The hall, where old clock
Chimes the hours,
Old chest with boul
Of lavender flowers.

That scent the hall
And draw me in,
Small window there and
Light that's dim.

So much forgotten
Life away,
Across the world
Our feet will stray.

But to that lovely
Childhood space,
I shall return
And leave life's race.

For me the rest
Can be forgot,
But never that dear
Hallowed plot.

The place where once
We children played,
The house, the lane,
The woodland glade.

Unchanged and sweet
In God's own hand,
My home,
The place I understand.

WHO CARES

They've put a by-pass round our town
A thousand trees have all come down,
Protesters came from far and near
To save the woodland held so dear.

Respectable stands our country town
Well shod feet walk up and down.
"Ah yes, a by-pass", so they say,
"Will take the traffic noise away."

Respectable . . . but just yesterday
I happened to walk along the way,
By the Park Gates, beneath the rail
I saw an old man lying frail.

Only the pavement for his bed
Newspaper pillows for his head,
Frost hard at night, or maybe rain
Wet dripping walkway, flooded drain.

Old sack was wrapped about his head
A dirty blanket for his bed,
Round carrier bag his fingers curled
His only treasure in this world.

Four million has the bypass cost
A thousand trees cut down and lost,
But what the cost if spent instead
To provide that old man with dry bed?

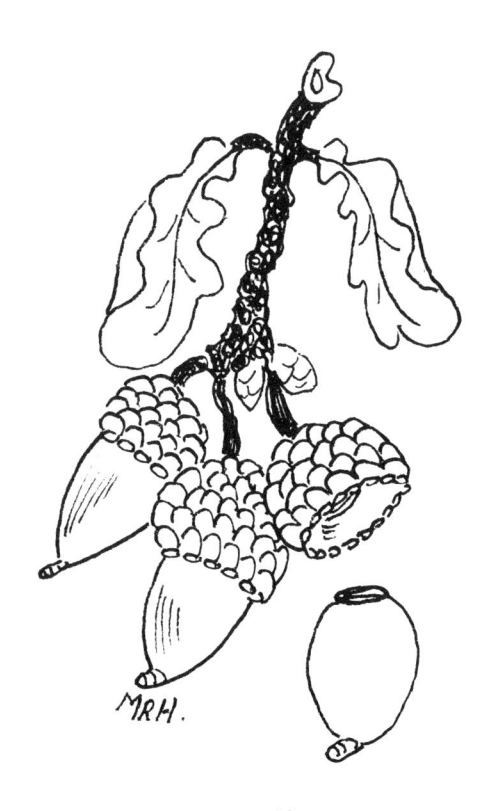

DAFFODILS BLOWING

Daffodils blowing, Springs on the way
Catkins are nodding, warmer each day,
Grass on the hillside, is growing Spring green
Oak buds are opening, dainty pink sheen.

Velvet faces of pansies by my cottage door
Squirrels are waking, to chase woodland floor,
Wild ducks are nesting in old willows hole
Earth mounds in meadow, from old Mr. Mole.

Old Bowker is digging, and planting his seeds
The moorhens are building among the green reeds,
The hedges are green, along the ploughed field.
Michael Gold rolls his meadow to nurture it's yield.

The spikes of wild arum are in Dumble Wood
And primrose are flowering, where old cottage stood,
Such joy every morning when all the birds sing
And daffodils blowing; at last comes the Spring.

BADDESLEY CLINTON

A house at peace amongst the trees
Where history whispers on the breeze,
Time trodden bridge across the moat
Rustling the reeds where white swans float.

Gate-house to inner garden court
Flower beds in coat of arms are wrought,
Clematis drapes the moat-side wall
Wysteria-hung the gatehouse tall.

Here door of oak and panelled wall
And ancient table grace the hall,
Here sunshine warms the window sills
And coloured glass the history spells.

Time has smoothed the strains away
Strife ridden times of yesterday,
When Catholics hid within the house
And floor boards harboured more than mouse.

Then anxious Ferrers risked their lives
Sad dangerous times for Clinton wives,
Cover of darkness; riders send,
No one shall know them; foe or friend.

Priest hole lies hidden, secret place
Dark cloak conceals a thin white face,
Black is the water, moonlight gleams
Mellow the brick, silver the steam.

Only the yeoman dawn reaping his hay
Watches the priest slip quiet away,
But wisely the yeoman turns his head
Sharpens his sickle blade instead.

Now in the sunshine of today
All the sad ghosts have passed away,
We try to imagine, believe, and guess
At best, it is only fancy dress.

Only the ghosts of long ago
Only her sleeping dead can know,
'The Trust' are her wardens, cherish with care,
Our pride in the coat of arms she bear.

EXHALL IN MAY

Cherry petals blow the pavements
Snowstorms in the Month of May,
Exhall village gave me welcome
Artist's paintings on display.

Crafts and pictures for your pleasure
Village hall for cheese and wine,
Local talent shares it's treasure
Hanging space for yours and mine.

Bobbin-lace is on the pillow
Landscape church to catch my eye,
Phyllis Cobley's patchwork quilting
A lovely owl, dark-framed and shy.

Friendships formed with one another
Money raised for Christian Aid,
Little showers and Springtime sunshine
Remembers all the friends I made.

Bluebells line the Churchyard pathway
Family service packs each pew,
Hymns of joy we joined in singing
Happiness for me and you.

Village life held dear and homely
Above the coal left in the mine,
Across the fields M6 goes racing
But Exhall's safe . . . . in arms devine.

OPEN YOUR EYES

Open your eyes to be sunshine
To the wind that rustles the corn,
Open your eyes to the blue of the sky
And the dew on the roses at dawn.

Open your eyes to the Springtime
The daffodils blow in the grass,
The violets, the primrose, the bluebells,
When Winter has faded at last.

Open your eyes to the moonlight
Soft fingered as gentle dreams,
Silvers the trees and the hedgerows,
Silvers the running stream.

Open your eyes to the garden
The perfume and colours are there,
The scent of lavender crushed in your hand,
The wonderful joys that we share.

Open your eyes to the sea-shore
The waves that ripple the sand,
The cliffs, and the sky, and the gulls flying high,
Above this most beautiful land.

Open your eyes to our children
Trusting small hands reach for mine,
Show them the trees, and the hills and the sea,
The gifts that are all life's sweet wine.

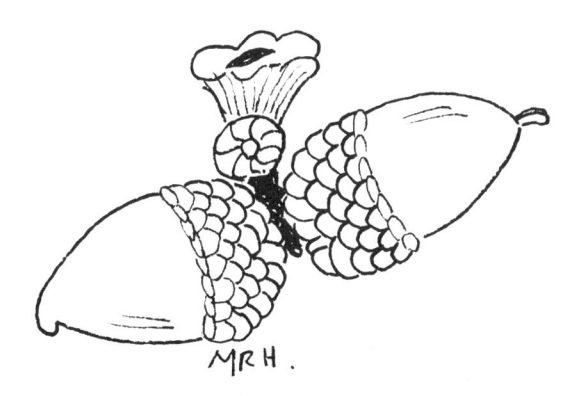

MY GARDEN

The meadow belongs to the daisy
The lark's nest, the clover, the bee,
The long grass gives home to the fieldmouse
  But the garden belongs to me.

The mountain belongs to the heather
The rocks, and the wind off the sea,
The sheep and the lambs on the hillside
  But the garden belongs to me.

The woodland belongs to the badger
And the squirrel that lives in the tree
The woodowls that hunt in the forest
  But the garden belongs to me.

The cornfield belongs to the harvest
Where the poppy blows scarlet and free,
With the wheat, and the oats and the barley
  But the garden belongs to me.

The marshland belongs to the wild geese
And the birds that fly in from the sea,
The redshank, the snipe and the mallard
  But the garden belongs to me.

The river belongs to the otter
A swimmer most excellent he,
Blue king-fishers over the water
  But the garden belongs to me.

The woodland, the moor, and the mountain,
Are there for wild things to run free,
The hedgehog, the deer and the rabbit
  But God, . . . made my garden for me.